One Lung *to* Live

*How a Tragedy Produces Inspiration & Life Lessons
That Will Help You Become the Best Version of
Yourself*

Tashell Williams, CWC

Dedication

To my grandmother Alphretta..

Words alone could never express what you mean to me. You gave me the best gift I could ever have... an introduction to Jesus. My life would not be what it is today if it wasn't for you. Thank you for always believing in me and loving me with the heart of Christ. You have always been my safe space to breathe and feel free to be me without judgement. You know and understand the layers of my being, bringing me ultimate peace and comfort. Thank you for being my healthy soil where I am planted and continuing to grow. I thank God for you daily!

To my husband, Chris..

Your unconditional love and belief in me have once again pushed me to do something I never thought about doing. This time, it's one of the greatest things I have ever done!

To my children Tamiah, Taylor, Tre & Cadence..

You all have taught me how to love and how to give birth to something beautiful that makes the world a better place.

You all are my inspiration and motivation to be a better version of myself daily.

There is a story to tell because of your marvelous existence.

Use this story as your road map to God's perfect plan and purpose for your life.

I Love You All,

Tashell

CONTENTS

Introduction

What do you think is the most valuable part of you? Your material possessions? How much money you have in the bank? Your social status? No! It's your story! God left me here on this earth to give you the most valuable part of me... My story! Never in a million years would I have thought I would be sharing such a unique story about my life, let alone think it was something worthy enough to put into a book. I am a numbers girl, not a writer.

As much as I want to say this book is so late compared to when this story happened, I have to say that it's right on time!

My husband and I just recovered from a horrible fight with COVID. As I laid there day after day looking at the ceiling, wondering if it was my time to depart from this earth, one of the things that kept me fighting was the fact that I had not told the world my testimony and all of the lessons I learned from it!

When I was out of the woods, I grabbed my computer and began to pour out this powerful story of what God has done in my life.

Get ready for a mind-blowing, inspiring, and life-changing story!

Enjoy!

CHAPTER 1

THE UNEXPECTED HAPPENED

It was hot and sticky on a rainy day as I sat in a classroom at Texas Southern University. Out of all days, the air conditioner had gone out, and they decided to raise the windows... uugghhh I never could stand that muggy feeling from when the humidity makes its way into the room. Something was different about this "muggy day"... it felt like the air was literally being sucked out of the room. It was if I was fighting to get a puff of oxygen to fill my lungs. As unfamiliar as that felt, it was familiar.. Months prior, during the summer of 2000, I was at Katy Mills shopping with Taylor (my daughter), who was seven months at the time. I remember that same feeling when I got in the car. The feeling was like the air was being sucked out of the car. I told my momma about it and blamed it on Houston's heat that I always jokingly claimed to be "allergic" to. My momma suggested that I go to the doctor to get checked out, but being hard-headed and young, I did not. So here we go again with this scary feeling of not being able to breathe. I decided to get up and drive to my parents' house to get some relief somehow, so I thought. Normally on the journey to my parents' house from Texas Southern, I am very cautious because there are a lot of cops sitting in certain spots waiting to give tickets. This day the more I drove, the more my chest got tighter, the more my anxiety kicked in, the more I thought to myself, "I can't breathe!" I thought I was going to pass out while I was driving. Through my shallow breaths, my eyes were darting from left to right frantically because I was looking for the police officer usually sitting at the overpass. I needed to pull over to him so that he could help me. Thank God he was sitting in his typical spot! I pulled over to him, rolled my window down and barely got out the words, "I can't breathe." He reacted immediately! He called the ambulance and my momma. When the ambulance arrived, they put an oxygen mask on my face, checked my vitals, and began a series of questions trying to figure out what was causing my shortness of breath. By then, my momma had also arrived, which gave me so much peace. My vitals were fine, and my oxygen levels increased to normal levels with the oxygen they gave me. They wanted to release me at that moment, but my momma told them to take me to the hospital because I had complained about having an episode like this before. She specifically told them to take me to St. Luke's Hospital, so that is what they did. That ride in the ambulance was a first of mine. I do not remember it much because my mind was going crazy trying to figure out what could be happening to me. When I got to St. Luke's, they did blood work, EKG, and an x-ray. The blood work and EKG came back normal. The only thing we were waiting on was the results from my chest x-ray. I will never forget the doctor walking up to us and saying, "There is something abnormally large on your right lung. You should see your PCP right away." They didn't think it was anything serious because I was so young. However, they wanted me to get further testing.

CHAPTER 2

THE WRONG DIAGNOSIS

I made an appointment hastily with my Primary Care Physician (PCP) Dr. Richard Carney. He is an extraordinary, wise, and thorough doctor I love and respect dearly. I remember him sitting with his perfectly combed hair, freshly ironed coat, with his legs crossed, showing off his shiny loafers, listening patiently to me explain my experience. He had a confused look on his face during our visit as I could tell that his mind was moving 1000 miles per hour, trying to figure out what the heck was going on with me. He started on his quest to find a solution to the problem by sending me to receive a CAT Scan. The CAT Scan was painless, but it was also a first for me. I was hoping that they found nothing seriously wrong with my results. My nerves were bad the next couple of days as I anxiously waited for my CT results.

One morning, I finally got a call from Dr. Carney's office, but I was in class, and they left a message telling me to call them back. When I called them back, the line was busy. Uuugghhhh.. I had to go to my next class. Of course, the office called again while I was in class, and I missed the call. On the way home from class, I finally got someone on the phone. I think my heart stopped when I heard the nurse's voice. The nurse said, "I need to speak with your mother to share your results." I said, "Why is that? I am 22 years old" I almost got mad because I just wanted her to hurry up and tell me my results so I could be at ease. She then said," The upper part of your right lung is collapsed, and we don't know why. We need you to see a pulmonary specialist right away. Here is your referral." As soon as Nurse Linda said those words to me, I could not breathe! This time it was due to anxiety. My body was malfunctioning! I was so scared, nervous, and shocked. I was speechless! I felt like I was going to pass out at that moment because I kept forgetting to breathe. I thought to myself, "I have a collapsed lung? Is something really wrong with me? How can this be happening to me? But I am so young and healthy." As my anxiety began to build, I hung up with Nurse Linda. I immediately called Dr. Herlihy's office to schedule an appt. for a bronchoscopy (which is when they stick a tube with a camera on the end of it down your throat to see what is going on) and biopsy. Upon meeting Dr. Herlihy, what stood out to me was that he looked very young to be a doctor. My nerves took over because I had no clue what to expect this bronchoscopy experience to be like, so I was preparing myself. They had already told me I had to get put to sleep for this procedure which made me uneasy because it would be my first time. Cheers to a lot of first times because I knew it was necessary to find out what was wrong with me.

After changing into my gown and getting an IV inserted into my arm, I woke up not remembering what happened at all. I felt queasy, nauseous, and really out of it. I felt like I was in a dream, some parts were blurry and some were clear. The clear part was the confused look on Dr. Herlihy's face as he told my mom what he had found. He found a tumor blocking the airway of my right lung, which is what caused the upper part of my right lung to be collapsed. He collected a biopsy of the tumor and sent it off to pathology. Although my momma didn't tell me this for a very long time, she said he told her that the tumor was cancerous. She questioned how he knew right after the biopsy, and his response was, "I know it when I see it." She asked him not to tell me until he got the results from the biopsy and was sure that it was cancer. Days later, he got the biopsy results, and it was NOT cancer; it was called a

Granular Cell tumor. We were so happy it was not cancer; however, this tumor was extremely rare in medicine. Instead of appearing as a ball or solid like most tumors, it was described as being gooey and can spread like cancer. Due to the tumor's rarity, he referred us to MD Anderson Hospital. Even though the diagnosis was wrong initially, I Thank God he sent us to the right place!

CHAPTER 3

THE RIGHT PLACE

Things moved pretty quickly because my case was considered severe. October 2nd was my 1st appointment at MD Anderson Hospital. As nervous as I was, the fact that it was my sister LaQuette's birthday made me feel some sort of comfort. My momma and I pulled up to MD Anderson, and I remember still feeling like I was in a dream. I had heard so many great things about MD Anderson; my Aunt Vee even worked there and loved it! Never in a million years would I have thought I would be a patient there. I did not quite know what to expect, but here we were. We valeted the car and walked in, searching for the elevator. This place was huge! The first thing I saw was the aquariums full of beautiful fish! The ambiance was warm and cozy, like a lived-in home. The smell of fresh coffee filled the air. I saw lots of people walking swiftly in all directions. Some people had on scrubs, white coats, regular clothes, etc. As I stood there taking it all in, I thought to myself," So this is the famous place where lives are saved?" I felt a sense of safety that my life was in the right hands. We looked around for the elevators, and we learned that there were many sets of elevators, so we had to find the ones that would take us to where we needed to be. We got on the elevator and went to Floor 9, the Thoracic Unit, signed in, and took a seat. I got a little nervous as we sat there waiting. While we were sitting there, an older sweet lady with a name tag that read "volunteer" rolled her cart over to us and offered us complimentary snacks and coffee, which we gladly accepted. "That was so nice of her," I thought to myself. It slightly helped my nervousness. Shortly after, the nurse opened the door from the back and said, "Tashell Miles?" as she slowly looked around the waiting room. My heart dropped, but I waved my hand in the air so she could see I was there, and we got up and followed her to my examination room.

On the walk back to the room, I felt like everything was in slow motion; I turned my head from left to right as I could see people in their examination rooms on both sides of the hall of all ages and races. In some weird way, seeing those people made me feel like I was not on this journey alone. I exhaled. I said a prayer for them and walked into my room, anticipating the meeting of my new doctor. I sat down on the white paper that neatly covered the exam table and looked around the room. It was a nice-sized room with a sink, a stool, and an extra chair for visitors. It was sterile, but it gave the consistent feeling of coziness. Not long after that, a Nurse Practitioner walked in to go over my medical history, then (drum roll please) Dr. Garrett Walsh walked in! My initial thoughts were, "Wow, he also looks young to be a doctor. I wonder how long he has been practicing? He must be a great doctor if he is at MD Anderson.." He was tall with brown hair and tight eyes wearing a white medical coat. He introduced himself to both my momma and me, and we had a very light conversation about our worlds that had nothing to do with what I was there to do. I honestly needed that more than I realized.

I learned that he was from Canada (he had a bit of an accent), his wife was a nurse, and he had kids. We had a few commonalities, one, in particular, being that one of his children was around the same age as Taylor. We shared stories, and before long, my nerves dissipated. At that point, I had a good feeling about him. His presence had calming energy. He then began to talk about the issue at hand. "This tumor." He was so surprised at my age, meaning I was only 22, facing this kind of health challenges, and even more blown away about the rarity of the granular cell tumor. He asked me questions regarding my parents or anyone in my family smoking, etc. He was trying to figure out from where this tumor came. To conclude our appt., he ordered tests, which consisted of an X-Ray, Blood Work, Cat Scan, and another Bronchoscopy...uughhhh I did not want to do that again! After receiving the results, he went into problem-solving and research mode of getting rid of the tumor and saving the remaining part of my lung. He suggested radiation, chemotherapy, and general medication as methods to shrink the tumor. So I went to 3 doctors, one for chemotherapy, one for radiation, and one for general medication, to see if they could improve my circumstance. It all took place in one month. I was declined to do any of the treatments because of the risk of damaging too many good cells. The remaining solution was to surgically remove the tumor.

All this time, Dr. Walsh had been researching worldwide to find history on this type of tumor located in the lung and could not find it. He told me that because of the location of the granular cell tumor that there was a 50/50 chance of survival. Even though that information was alarming, Dr. Walsh was so comforting about the surgery that I wasn't afraid to have it. I just really wanted to be healthy, so I could continue to live life. We checked calendar dates to see what date would be best so I would not miss too much school, and BAM, it was settled. We decided to have my surgery on December 13th, 2000, during the Christmas Holiday break to recover for two weeks and be back in class for the spring semester at Texas Southern University.

CHAPTER 4

THE SURGERY

The surgery… As I think back, I can't believe I was so courageous and unafraid to have such a serious surgery. I definitely know that God was with me and my faith was totally in Him.

Ok, back to the story..

I was so excited to have this surgery so I could be back in school for the spring semester and carry on with my life with Taylor! I was told I would be back to normal in two weeks! To prepare, I made sure Taylor would be in good hands with my loving grandmother. I went and got braids (1st time), so I wouldn't have to deal with my hair, and I got my nails and feet "done". I guess I wanted to be cute while recovering in the hospital. Lol, I also made sure I had all the CDs I wanted to listen to on my portable cd player. I couldn't be in one room for two weeks without some good inspirational music. One of my favorite gospel artists at the time was Yolanda Adams, so I absolutely had her cd on the list. My momma asked me a couple of times if I knew who would care for Taylor if something happened to me. I was so irritated by her asking me that. I snapped and got defensive each time because I didn't want to think about the negative risks of the surgery. I felt at peace...My momma's peace of mind also encouraged me to find before my surgery, and I did not want to welcome fear into that experience. I know that she had good intentions; she wanted me to take care of my business since I was a new mother and young adult.

Dec. 13, 2000, finally arrived! I got dressed in my favorite overalls I wore when I was pregnant with Taylor, grabbed my overnight bag, and headed to MD Anderson. We arrived at the waiting room and checked in. I was in awe of how many people were waiting to have surgery. There were older and younger people. I could feel the uneasy and fearful energy in the waiting room. It felt cold, no one was smiling, and everyone had similar looks of sadness. My family (momma & 2 dads) waiting with me made me feel like I was waiting to have a tooth removed. The conversation, LOL, was light and comforting. I danced around (like usual) and periodically checked my bag to make sure I had packed everything I needed, especially my CDs. I couldn't be without my music, can you tell? Every time the nurse opened the door and called a name, I jumped up with anticipation hoping it was mine. I was so ready to be "fixed"! (Door Opens) "Tashell Miles," the nurse announced. "Yes, that's me!" I said. They only let one person accompany me to the back, so my momma grabbed her purse and came with me. When I got to the prep area, a nurse handed me a gown and told me to change into it so I would be comfortable. When I came back into the waiting area, the nurse led me to a bed where my momma was sitting. It was like being in an emergency room where the two curtains were on each side that separated me from the other patients. The nurse told me that anesthesia would be there in a couple of minutes to get me prepped for surgery. When anesthesia arrived, she said she would give me an epidural to numb the upper part of my body. I immediately froze in fear. I didn't know what to expect with this surgery, but I knew what it was like to have an epidural because I had just had one a year ago when I was in labor with Taylor. As I got myself together for this needle being inserted into my back, I noticed the anesthesiologist took a long time to stick me. She fumbled and acted as if she was unsure about what she was doing. My momma noticed it as well and quickly said, "Is something wrong?" The anesthesiologist replied, "No, nothing is wrong. I am a new anesthesiologist." Oh my goodness, why did she tell us that? Lol, My momma then suggested another anesthesiologist give me my epidural because she was uncomfortable with how this one was acting. Lol Gotta love my momma.. The new anesthesiologist administered my epidural flawlessly. The last thing I remember is being kissed by both dads on each cheek, then being rolled away to surgery.

In my surgery, the goal was to remove the Granular Cell tumor from my airway and save the remaining part of my right lung, but when they opened me up, the doctors found something they didn't expect to see. The Granular Cell tumor had grown so aggressively (in two months) that it glued itself to my spine and vocal cords, grew up my main airway and cut off all oxygen to my right lung. I read in my report that Dr. Walsh and the other doctors had to stop and consult in the middle of surgery because what they saw was so unexpected and rare. They decided to do something that had NEVER BEEN DONE before... remove my entire right lung (because it was no longer functioning) AND a portion of my main airway and re-attached it to my left lung. I lost a lot of blood and had to get a blood transfusion. The doctors were surprised that I made it through the surgery! To God be all the glory I did, but I wasn't out of the woods just yet.

CHAPTER 5

THE FIGHT OF MY LIFE

After surgery, my momma said I was doing well until the 3rd day in ICU. I took a major turn for the worst. My oxygen levels dropped critically low, so I was placed in a medically induced coma and was put on a ventilator for a month and a half, which was way longer than normal. While on the ventilator I experienced everything you could name, even death, twice! I had one complication after another. Per my report I had postoperative ARDS, respiratory failure, pneumonia, sepsis, cardio pulmonary arrest two times, c. difficile colistis, a uti and left pneumothorax. I was literally in T H E F I G H T O F M Y L I F E as I laid in that ICU bed. I had very resistant pneumonia, so I was put on multiple compounded antibiotics.. I had chest tubes, central lines, a tube feeding up my nose, and so many bags of medication and fluids going into my body. I was so critical that they put me in a "prone" position to increase my oxygen saturation. To be in a prone position means that I was placed on my stomach, hoping that my oxygen level would improve. Eighty percent of patients put in prone positions eventually die. My family often gathered to pray because Dr. Walsh stated I was so ill, but he never gave up on me. As time passed, I got many visits from my family, friends, pastors, other patients' families, etc., which I don't remember. My momma was the "gatekeeper" of my stay in ICU. She never let anyone see me that was crying because she knew I could hear even though I was in a coma. She didn't want me to lose faith or hope that I would pull through. She was very particular about who prayed for me, etc. I had friends who told me stories about them sneaking into ICU at all hours of the night and lying about being kin to me to visit me. Honestly, I feel like everyone that witnessed me in the fight of my life was impacted more than I was at the time. I can only imagine the plethora of emotions felt by each person who laid eyes on me. I can only imagine what my momma and daddy felt from day to day, taking this unpredictable roller coaster of a journey with me. I feel like I was asleep while God healed my body for all to see.

The Crazy Dream

While in my coma, I had an odd dream. I dreamt I was alone in the backseat of a parked car. I was paralyzed with my eyes closed. However, I could see myself having some sort of out-of-body experience. It was raining cats and dogs, and the sun was shining. Then there appeared in the car with me a skunk, yes a skunk! It was crawling all around the car and over my lap. The rule was if the skunk sprayed you, you would die. The skunk climbed onto my lap and sprayed me in the face. I passed out, but I woke up. When I woke up, family members and friends were standing in the rain, looking into the car at me. Some were trying to get the doors open, and others were crying. Then the skunk climbed onto my lap again and sprayed me in the face. Once again, I passed out, but I woke up. When I woke up this time, more family and friends were standing around the car helplessly trying to get me out.

The rain pour was even harder than before. This encounter with the skunk happened one more time. I passed out but woke up, but this time, the sun was shining, and my family and friends had smiles on their faces, and no one was trying to open the doors to get me out. It was like all was well with the world.. The End. I didn't know this was a dream until... After waking up, I asked my momma, through lip talking,

"What happened to the skunk?" She looked at me with a confused look and said, "What skunk?" "Nevermind," I replied. I thought I had gone crazy. I have a great idea of what that dream symbolized.

Waking Up

I don't remember when I "woke up" exactly; however, I remember some things about my stay in ICU in no particular order.

I remember..

Realizing that I had missed my favorite time of the year.. Christmas. I had a little Christmas stocking with my name on it on my bed. My momma said they delivered them when I was in my coma.

I remember..

My wrists were tied to the bed because my momma said I would try to pull my breathing tube out of my mouth.

I remember..

Realizing that I was too weak to move or do anything for myself. I didn't understand why that was the case. They told me I had lost majority of my muscle mass (strength) from lying in bed without movement for so long.

I remember..

Always being so uncomfortable in my bed no matter what. I was so thin that it hurt to lay still in one spot too long. To ease the pain, I asked to be turned (change positions) and for extra pillows to prop me up. Typically 1-2 people would have to turn me. My momma had seen it so much that she started to help in this process.

I remember..

I could not talk due to the breathing tube down my throat, so I used my hands to point to a handheld board with alphabets, numbers and pictures to communicate. My hands would shake uncontrollably, trying to do something as simple as pointing to pictures.

I remember..

The resounding rattle of fluid in my chest when I needed to be suctioned triggered my horrendous cough.

I remember..

Going as long as I could without coughing because my cough took so much energy out of me. My entire body shook! A hard cough made me feel like I was coughing up my remaining lung. Every time I coughed, I fought the urge to vomit...sometimes, I didn't win..

I remember..

Needing a nurse, but being too weak to press the call button.

I remember..

I had a bedpan in which the nurses would slide under my butt go to the restroom. What a humbling experience.

I remember..

My momma and the nurses kept my portable cd player with Yolanda Adams' music on my ears. Her music became my inspiration and soundtrack during my hospital stay.

I remember..

Having difficulty sleeping at night because my days and nights were all mixed up. There was not a window in my room, which I know contributed to the confusion.

I remember..

The nurses gave me shots around the clock. It seemed like the shots in my stomach and hips would never come to an end. It kept me from getting good sleep.

I remember..

My stomach swelled up like I was pregnant, and I felt so overfed and uncomfortable. Come to find out, there was an issue with my feeding tube. Dr. Walsh (I love him) gave the nurses instructions on how to fix the issue over the phone while he was in Canada on Christmas vacation with his family.

I remember..

My temperature changing from hot to cold and cold to hot in a matter of minutes. I kept a fan in my room and heavy blankets on my bed. Whenever I needed the blankets put on me or taken off of me, my nurse or momma would have to do it for me because I was too weak to do it myself.

I remember..

Taylor's pictures from birth to present lined up alongside my bed so I could see them at all times.. She was my motivation to live! My "why"!

I remember..

My family members would come to see me and cry behind my bed, so that I could not see them, but little did they know, I could hear them. My Aunt Vee (who works for MD Anderson) would sneak over to see me and not come in the room because she couldn't stand to see me so ill.

I remember..

My momma told me that my Aunt Kim would call from her trip (she is a flight attendant) crying.

I remember..

My momma said my grandmother was crying, saying that I didn't deserve to go through what I was going through.

I remember..

The laborious work of being weaned off the ventilator. It was so painful to take EVERY single breath because the lung muscle is so hard to rehabilitate. I would beg my respiratory therapist to put me back on the ventilator because of the excruciating pain. "No" was ALWAYS the answer..

I remember..

Having my favorite respiratory therapists that suctioned my airway without making me gag and having the not-so-favorite ones that were extremely rough and brought me to tears.

I remember..

My nurses helped me sit up in the bed, moved my legs to hang on the side of the bed and lifted me to a standing position. Then they would sit me down in a chair on the side of my bed to help me regain my strength. I dreaded this time of the day. I know that sounds like a simple task, but it was SO HARD after lying in bed for so long! When anyone entered the room, I would pat my bed as a sign that I wanted to lay back down. They told me "No" to that too.

I remember..

Dreading my sheets being changed because to roll me from one side of the bed to the other would cause me to be dizzy and vomit. It felt like being on a roller coaster which I have never been fond of.

I remember..

They ran out of places to put an IV because I had been stuck so many times.

I remember..

Learning to embrace "ICU" baths, especially from one of my nurses that was pregnant. She moved so slowly that it kept me freezing cold the whole time but afterward felt like I had hit the jackpot as soon as the warm blankets touched my skin.

I remember..

One of my favorite respiratory therapists called me "sunshine". His way to encourage me when challenging times came was always to remind me that I needed to get home to Taylor and start dancing again.

I remember..

My momma greased me up and down with Vaseline from my lips to my feet. It's amazing how dry your skin gets in the hospital. I didn't have one bedsore after lying in bed for two months.

I remember..

The funny moments of lip talking to my momma and her inability to read my lips. She would always think I was saying something way off from what I was really saying. Lol

I remember..

The daily visits from Dr. Walsh were the highlight of my day. He always made me feel optimistic about my progression.

I remember..

The TV being a blur even with my glasses on.

I remember..

Waiting for the procedure to insert a central line.

I remember..

Thinking, "Am I pregnant?" Because I never had a cycle the whole time.

I remember..

Every morning, I would ask the nurse to call my momma to ask her when she was coming up to the hospital. I would bug them until she came. Her presence always made me feel better.

I remember being so determined to do everything I could to go home.

Dr. Walsh gave me a goal to hit, to move one step closer to being discharged. He told me if I got weaned from the ventilator and took two steps during Physical Therapy, I could be transferred from ICU to a regular hospital room (The Ward). I remember the excitement I got when Physical Therapy would come to get me up out of bed, moving me around every day. Every time they came, I believed this was my chance to walk two steps and hit my goal! Sometimes I would be so excited that my blood pressure would be so high that I could not do PT. So disappointing.. I was soooo determined to get better! After sweat, tears, and much determination, I willed my tiny body to walk two steps! Yeeees! It was time to move to The Ward! The transfer to The Ward was a celebratory parade in which they attached balloons to my bed and wheeled me around the ICU unit for everyone to see me, applaud, cheer and wish me well! Even though I was so ready to get out of ICU, it was bittersweet.. I saw faces with smiles and some with tears. I left a special place with amazing people that I would never forget. They fought the fight of my life right alongside me. I know they all loved me and cared for me beyond what they were paid to do. Without them, I wouldn't have made it. Those nurses, respiratory therapists, doctors, and assistants had become my family, and ICU had become my home.

CHAPTER 6

ONE STEP CLOSER TO HOME

So here I was being wheeled into my new room…one step closer to going home! It had been exactly 48 hours since I was last on a ventilator. Might I add that those were the worst 48 hours of my life! I was breathing on my own even though I still felt ill and had very little strength. I wondered just how much change I would encounter in two weeks before I went home. I still needed a lot of assistance.

When we slowly rolled into the room, I noticed the natural light shining through the window! It was as if it was giving me its' own welcome. I didn't know how much natural light mattered until I spent that time in ICU without it. It made me feel happy and hopeful about my recovery!

Things during this time are somewhat of a blur, but here are some things I remember..

I remember..

The only time I would feel sick to my stomach was when the nurse would give me medication. It was like my body was rejecting everything from the pharmacy.

I remember..

My cough was a little better, so I didn't have a respiratory therapist to suction me as often, and they didn't have to go as deep into my chest. Thank God! I had my suction tube attached to the side of my bed to dispose of my mucus when I coughed. It was very similar to the suction tube that the dentist uses when cleaning your teeth. As much as I needed to cough everything up to continue to get better, I also felt uncomfortable doing that when I had visitors. I thought the suction sounds and seeing my mucous would gross them out.

I remember..

I got a visit from some special friends I graduated with from Second Baptist High School.. To see their faces meant the world to me, even though their faces were covered with concern and forced smiles.

I remember..

My only friend who could relate to me in this new body came to visit me. Tawana Malbrough, Lord rest her soul, came to see me amid her health challenges. She was a cancer survivor and lived with one lung. I was so happy to see her, especially because she often didn't leave her home due to her health challenges. I don't remember much about our visit, but I remember being in awe of her as she shared that she had gotten into nursing school. She was my inspiration that I could one day live a "normal" life again. If she could do it, so could I!

I remember..

The excitement that built from ICU to now about talking again. I think I was more excited about talking than I was about eating. Lol, It's amazing how I took for granted the ability to use my voice to communicate. For me to speak again, the hole made in my throat for my breathing tube had to be closed. I couldn't wait to hear how I sounded. The day finally came when this procedure would happen.. Yes! I thought to myself, "I finally get to hear my voice! I wonder if I can still sing. What in the world was I going to sound like?" Singing was a big part of my life. The procedure was short and sweet as the nurse deadened my neck, stitched it up, and put a band-aid on it. When I opened my mouth to talk, you wouldn't believe what came out! Out came my new voice, which was breathy and strained. Before surgery, my voice was raspy and strong, but my new voice was a hoarse whisper...I was so confused and disappointed. "Why does my voice sound like this?" I asked my nurse. She told me that one of my vocal cords was damaged due to being intubated for longer than usual and because I had not used my voice in such a long time. Due to a decrease in lung capacity, the volume of my voice would be lower than usual. Even though I was surprised by the sound of my voice, I still was happy about hearing it. I was very hesitant about using it for a while because talking would cause me to go into a body- shaking coughing tantrum, which often ended in me gagging and trembling with a face full of tears. The cough would make me feel like the band-aid that was holding the stitches in my neck from the tracheostomy together was going to pop off.

I remember..

The day I had my tube feeding removed from my nose to eat something finally. I wasn't that hungry, but I was ready to eat. Because I did not know what to expect, I asked numerous times if this procedure would be uncomfortable because EVERYTHING was uncomfortable. The answer given was always "No." I hoped that they were telling the truth and not just saying what would make me not be afraid. On that day, the nurse sat on a stool right beside my bed, told me to lean forward towards him, and tilt my head back so he could reach the tube in my nose. He began to pull the tube from my nose slowly. I felt like he was slowly pulling my insides out through my nose. I was gagging uncontrollably, so my eyes leaked, and salty tears saturated my face. If I had it my way, I preferred he pull it out quickly to finish faster. As he got to the end of the tube, it stopped coming out, but it wasn't out of my nose. "Oh, no! What's going on?" I thought to myself. He pulled gently and tugged.. Still no movement. He pulled to the left, then to the right… Still no movement. At this point, I am moaning in unbearable pain and crying real tears because of it. It was obvious… This tube was stuck! He kept apologizing along the way but kept trying to wiggle this tube out of my nose. Then finally, it came out! I was so relieved! We looked closely at the end of the tube, and there was the issue…There was a knot that had formed at the end of the tube while it was in my stomach. The knot was stuck in my tiny nostril. Can you imagine the pain?

I remember..

The barium swallow test that I had to take before I could swallow any type of food or liquid. The nurse wheeled me down to a small room and handed me a super tall cup of white barium (liquid chalk) with a straw. The first thing I was going to swallow in 2 months was barium.. I was so excited! #not It tasted just like what it was... CHALK! It was hard to swallow, but I knew I had to do this to eat again. As I swallowed, they took pictures of the barium going down my throat. I would only be approved to eat or drink if I did not aspirate, which means the barium didn't go into my lung. I passed; however, I was told I had a delayed swallow.

I remember...

Dr. Walsh told me my next goal in order to go home. It was to walk around the whole nurse's station on a walker with assistance. I mean, was he crazy? I just took two steps to get into this room. For a person that couldn't walk, that seemed like a long walk. When Physical Therapy would get me moving, I went from being excited to dreading their presence. I was often in isolation, which meant I had to put on a yellow plastic gown, plastic gloves, and a mask over my face. Isolation was to protect me from the germs of others and to protect others from me. So when Physical Therapy came, they put on my smothering gear and helped me stand to hold on to the walker. Just rolling over, pulling my legs over to the side of the bed, and standing was a big and exhausting task.

I felt like I had flipped 10 of those large tires that people used to workout! My entire body shook like an old engine in a car because of my weak muscles. Two Physical Therapists, one on each side of me, would assist me as I took one slow step at a time. That was the most tiring thing to do EVER! With each step, I felt like I was going to fall out. No joke! My breathing was so rapid and shallow.. I could not catch my breath to get control of my breathing pace. At some point, I felt like the air in my lung didn't want to be there.. It was leaving my body for good. I just knew my heart would come out of my chest because of how hard it was beating. It didn't feel "right". It all felt wrong. Little did I know what I was experiencing was the usual recovery for a person who nearly died.

I remember..

When I got my chest tubes removed with a simple yank and stitches to follow, that was the easiest thing they had to do to prepare me for going home.

Discharge Time

Can you believe I was discharged without an oxygen machine or medication to take home with me? My doctors were in awe of me and called me a "Miracle"! Dr. Walsh told me that I was the only patient that came that close to death without dying. He also said that if I had not gotten my breathing checked out, I would have suddenly passed away within about three months because the tumor would have grown across my central airway without warning. Talk about a reality check of God's protection and plan for my life!! To God be all the glory for my healing!! He told me that I had a purpose that I needed to fulfill on this earth. A seed was planted when Dr. Walsh mentioned purpose. I began to think about what that meant in my life. I needed to know what God created me to accomplish for His glory. But first, let me tell you about my new normal.

CHAPTER 7

MY NEW NORMAL

I was discharged from the hospital on Feb 9, 2001. I was so happy to be on my way home to Taylor. I had anticipated this day since Dec. 13, 2000. My Aunt Kim and my momma came to pick me up. My momma brought clothes to put on besides the blueish-green gown I had been rocking for two months. Now I had moved on to a soft pajama set that was white with pink and green flowers and some plush house shoes. As small as that sounds, putting on something new to go home made my day. I had been through a lot; this represented new beginnings to me. As much as I looked forward to going home, I did not anticipate or expect the ride home. It was beyond rough.. Because I hadn't had much movement, I got motion sickness just to ride in a car. I was dizzy and extremely nauseous. I had to brace myself for every turn, stop, go and bump. When my Aunt Kim drove fast and slow, I cringed out of bodily confusion. My brain and my stomach were not on the same page. I didn't think the ride home

41

would be anything like this. I was depleted. When we pulled into the driveway at home as my head was spinning and I fought hurling, I thought about the last time I was there.. I was so excited, walking on my own, healthy for the most part, and weighing about 105 pounds. I had no clue how my life would change so drastically. Here I was two months later, weighing a frail 65 pounds, needing assistance to walk, barely talking and eating, BUT I was alive. When my grandmother opened the door with Taylor to greet me, I was overwhelmed with happiness. It was a moment I had been longing to see.. I was face to face with my motivation to fight to live...Taylor. My momma helped me slowly walk into the house step by step with my walker to avoid rapid breathing and coughing spells. My grandmother put some cushiony pillows on her leather couch for me to sit on so it would not feel like my tailbone would break through my thin skin. As I stood there waiting for her to do that, I felt comforted by the familiar smell of home. It was the smell I had been craving my entire hospital stay. My momma held my arm and slowly lowered me to sit as I gently bent my knees to sit down. They slid the ottoman close enough to connect with the couch and put my legs on top of it. My grandmother picked Taylor up, placed her on my lap, and held her steady. I was too weak and delicate to grab her by myself. I looked into her cute little face and was instantly filled with many emotions. I was sad, happy, excited, and scared simultaneously. I feared that Taylor would not remember me because I had been gone for so long, and I did not look like the momma she was familiar with, but she did. She looked at me and gave me the biggest smile and hug. As much as I tried to hold back my tears of excessive joy, they came flowing like a never-ending river. The thought of leaving Taylor on this earth without a mother crushed my heart. I was so thankful to God for saving my life and allowing me to continue the journey of being her mom. Even though I missed spending her 2nd Christmas with her, I was blessed to spend many more Christmases. Taylor (15 months) had grown so much in 2 months and walked and talked better than me.

The Simple Things

I needed assistance with EVERYTHING. It was like learning how to do everything all over again at the age of 22. I was given a bell to ring at my bedside for assistance since my voice was so soft, and I could not get up to do anything. The simple things weren't as simple for me anymore. I felt like a bother because I needed help doing everything! I had to ring the bell to have my blanket moved on and off my body and press the remote and telephone buttons. I was the phone queen before all of this, speaking of the phone. I loved talking on the phone for hours at a time, but now I could barely whisper. It took so much effort to get words out that I rarely spoke on the phone anymore. I got tired of hearing, "What did you say?" I was given an exercise regimen that consisted of small movements like extending my legs while I lay in bed, which completely exhausted me. I had 2-pound weights that I had to lift daily, and I couldn't do that for a while, and the times I did do it, it took an act of God to do it. I never knew anyone could be this weak, especially me.

To take a bath: My momma and grandmother installed a bench on the tub for me to sit on to bathe because my legs were so weak that I could not kneel. When I would kneel to a certain level, my legs would shake uncomfortably and give out. An ordeal that generally would take 30 mins would take about two hours from start to finish and leave me feeling like I just completed the iron man competition. After breathing hard and sweating, I honestly needed another bath afterward. I will never forget the smell of Caress soap from my 1st bath at home. When I got out of the shower, my momma helped me stand and dried me off. I got a full view of my body for the first time in 2 months.

I couldn't believe what I saw.. I looked like DEATH. My body had clearly been in a battle. I felt like someone had just taken a bat and knocked the wind out of me because it was so shocking. I had chest tube scars on both sides of my chest, scars from my central lines, and a trachea scar on my neck. My skin was hanging off of my bones to where I could see my ribs through my skin. I asked for another mirror so I could turn around and see the reflection of my back in the mirror. I saw the scar from where they removed my lung for the first time. The scar stretched from under my right arm and moved upward to the middle of my back. It was smooth, thick, and dark in color. It healed while I was in a coma; that's why I don't remember anything about the healing process. My face was sunken, my braids looked like locs, BUT the skin on my face was so smooth and without any blemishes. It was gorgeous, and I loved it. My teeth were perfect and straight because I had just gotten my braces taken off about nine months prior. I took a deep breath as my eyes scanned up and down and side to side as I processed my new body. I told my momma, "I will never show my body to anyone." She said, "Girl, just be glad you are alive!" She was right..

To walk: It took me hours to go from one room to another. I paused after every step contemplating if I wanted to take the next one. Whether I stood there or walked, I was in agonizing pain. I chose to take another step because it got me closer to sitting down, which relieved the pain. Not only was it hard to walk, but my arms were shaking from the weight I was putting on them. I used my walker and slowly moved around the house, shaking like a bag of bones while Taylor held my hand and "helped" me. She had an instinct to assist me, so she became one of my "nurses." Speaking of nurses, the great thing about coming home to my grandmother was that she is a retired nurse, so she knew exactly how to nurture me back to good health. God knew what I needed before I needed it.

To go to the bathroom: I needed help from my momma or grandmother to sit down and stand up from the toilet. One of them would grab me under my arm and slowly lower me to a seated position on the toilet. They tried not to cause discomfort, but it was inevitable because I was so fragile. I would use the toilet paper holder on the wall for support to stand back up in some cases. Thank God it never came out of the wall! It's amazing how the small muscles around the knees make such a difference in squatting and standing.

To eat: I had to take it slow, consume a liquid diet, and build up to solids because I hadn't had food in two months. I did not listen to that part on my 1st day home.. lol, I had my momma make me my favorite meal, which was spaghetti, and I threw up every bite. My goal was to gain weight to be healthier and look healthier. I didn't like looking so sickly. I hated looking in the mirror at myself. I ate soups and jello for a long time until I eventually took the leap of faith and tried solid foods. I slowly began to gain weight and get stronger taking one day at a time.

The Mental Challenge

As happy as I was to be living, my mental health began to decline. The phone calls and visits that were once so frequent stopped shortly after I got home. My relationships changed due to my condition. I leaned heavily on my friends for my happiness, an unrealistic expectation. Most of my friends were young adults living vibrant lives in college, working and having fun. Here I was struggling day by day to regain strength to walk, talk and do the basic things for myself that most children knew how to do. I fell out with a couple of friends because I wanted them to call and come to see me more. I didn't consider the effects that my current situation had on them. It probably was disturbing to see me in such an incapable state. They could not relate to what I was experiencing or had experienced. I had a strong desire for the company of my friends to laugh and connect like times before, even though it would have probably left me exhausted. I needed them to give me a break from my reality, even if it was just for a moment. I was silently losing it! I felt sad, helpless, and alone. I wanted everyone to care, but I felt like they didn't. My hair fell out and thinned tremendously, adding another layer of sadness. I always had healthy and long hair, so seeing that go away was heartbreaking. I cried out to God many times, "Why am I going through this?" Even though I masked it very well, I was so down in the dumps and flat-out depressed. I hid my tears. I was ashamed and felt a sense of guilt for feeling this way because, in my mind, I should have still been thanking and praising God for Him saving my life. Was I ungrateful? Why wasn't that enough to lift my spirits? I wasn't familiar with anxiety until this experience, and now I was full of it regarding things of the past and what was to come. The devil was so busy with my thoughts. "You couldn't breathe before; what if you can't breathe now? There is no machine here to save you.", were thoughts that came to my mind daily. Joy was around me, occupying space in my grandmother and Taylor, but it couldn't find its entryway into my heart. I felt stuck. My goal was to get back to being "normal," which wasn't happening fast enough.

The Physical Challenge

One day while I was frustrated, I asked my grandmother, "Grandmother, how do I go back to being able to walk again without assistance? I don't want to use this walker forever." She told me, "Stop using it and use the walls to get around the house. Just do it. Trust yourself and believe that you can do it even when it hurts. You will get stronger." I began to do what she told me to do. Day in and day out, I held on to the walls moving slowly like a turtle and breathing like a tired bear. It was strenuous! My heart would beat so fast it would scare me. I couldn't catch my breath often, and I felt as if I would pass out when I saw stars. Then on top of all of that, I would panic because it felt like I was going to die, and I was terrified! I realized I needed to change my expectations of recovery. Even though I didn't know what to expect, my goal was to sprint through this challenging time. I didn't want to stay limited, disabled, and need the help of others for too long. I caught on to the fact that this journey would be more of a marathon than a sprint. Some days I would stare at the ceiling because I didn't want to get up and do the work I needed to do consistently to get better. It felt like hell, and I was tired of the struggle! Most days, I didn't feel like going through the pain or being patient with myself to take forever just to walk around in my room or let alone into another part of the house. Then I would look at Taylor's smiling face and know that I needed to do it whether I felt like it or not. She depended on me to push through this. I was her momma, and it was my job to love her, protect her and steer her through life. She was my assignment from God, and I couldn't let them down. Even though everything hurt on my body because I was rebuilding the most of my muscles, it took me hours to move around the house, and I was dizzy and scared from my rapid breathing.. I got up every day.

I prayed and asked God to help me. I knew the only way to get through something this fatiguing was with Him by my side. I slowly began to shift my mindset to think more positively. I thought about and got thankful for what I could do versus being disgruntled and frustrated about the things I could not do. Every day when I woke up, I would close my eyes and envision what I was like before. It was like I was playing a mini-movie in my mind of what I wanted to be like again. I was walking around, laughing uncontrollably, dancing like no one was watching, singing my heart out, you name it. The more and more that happened, my hope cultivated, and my goals for myself became clear. I tracked my day-to-day activity and began to see my progression. Things that made me tired previously didn't wear me out as quickly. I was able to walk a little further every week. My muscles didn't shake as they did before, indicating that they were getting stronger. My belief in myself awakened as I saw myself get stronger every day. I was doing it!! I almost couldn't believe what was happening with my body. As I rehabilitated with a couple of visits to MD Anderson and at home for the 1st year, I had to make some significant physical adjustments in my lifestyle for my "new" body.

1) I had to slow down and pace myself. My energy levels were much lower than they were before. I was a roadrunner and a girl that loved to dance before this, so it was a big thing to slow down.

2) I couldn't lift anything heavy due to the doctor's orders.

3) I changed my eating habits. Since the doctors could not find out where my tumor came from, I decided to make better health choices, and it started with food. I eliminated beef and pork from my diet. Lord, I miss burgers!

4) I had to take my time swallowing to avoid choking because I had a delayed swallow due to my intubation. I choked a couple of times and thought I would see Jesus. I couldn't catch my breath and be seeing stars because I coughed so hard.

5) I adjusted to my heart palpitating because of its new location in my chest. Due to my lung expansion, it shifted to the right side of my chest.. The initial feeling of my heart palpitating scared the daylights out of me. It felt like my heart was about to stop beating, and it was giving me a warning.

6) I slept with a million pillows propping me up, or I would feel like I was suffocating. A couple of nights, I slid off of my pillows while sleeping, and I woke up gasping for air. It was a terrifying feeling!

7) I slept on my right side only because that's the best way oxygen flowed through my body. If I slept on my left side, I sounded like I was struggling to breathe because the weight didn't allow my lung to expand fully.

8) I drank out of a straw to control how fast liquid went down my throat to avoid choking. Even when I drank out of a straw, I would hold the fluid in my mouth and concentrate when I swallowed so I wouldn't choke.

9) I constantly made sure my posture was straight and not leaning toward the right because I had no support on the right side of my body. My grandmother would walk up behind me and shift my shoulders if she saw me leaning.

10) I had to remember to breathe correctly. I had to learn the "proper" way to breathe is from your diaphragm, not your chest. Breathing from my chest restricted my breathing and would send me into a panic attack.

11) I avoided strong smells because they made me short of breath. I ran from loud perfume/cologne, kitchens when food is fried, cleaning products

(especially bleach), strong candles, oil burners, and air fresheners. When I encountered them, I would go outside to fill my lung with fresh air. That made me feel better.

12) I covered my nose and mouth in freezing weather with a thick scarf or whatever I could grab because the cold air knocked the wind out of me.

13) I exercised more frequently, pushing myself to be out of breath because it made my lung capacity expand, which was a great thing.

14) I listened to my body and took as many naps as I needed to. I tended to get tired faster, so I rested to restore my energy as often as possible. That meant I learned to say no to the things in life that were not a necessity; I had to save my energy for the essential things.

15) My throat made a gurgling noise every time I swallowed. I was embarrassed by it, but it didn't bother me with time.

16) I accepted the new scars on my body that I tried so hard to keep flawless. My nurses in the hospital gave me suggestions on how to wear jewelry to cover my neck scars.

17) I no longer had the vocal range and volume I had before when I sang or spoke. So in loud environments, I typically couldn't be heard, so I stayed quiet, smiled upon eye contact, and waved. What a huge adjustment!

18) I could not yell at all due to my damaged vocal cord.

These adjustments and new things I had to learn to love and accept about myself did not happen overnight, and it was no walk in the park. At that time in my life, I wanted to fit in, be accepted, and be loved by others. This "NEW NORMAL" definitely made me STAND OUT. It made me even more insecure on many levels. I didn't like the way I looked and the extra steps I had to take just to LIVE. Was this really my New way of life?

CHAPTER 8

THE SPIRITUAL CHALLENGE

efore any of this happened, my spiritual life was vital to me. My spiritual journey started with attending Love United Methodist Church with my grandmother when I would go to her house on the weekends. I loved my grandmother and wanted to be just like her. If you were to walk into her church back in the 80s, she would be singing in the choir in the alto section. She was very active in serving the Lord in whatever capacity was needed. As a teenager, I accepted Christ as my personal Savior. I then branched off to my unique path of spirituality. I joined Willing Workers Missionary Baptist Church! If you were in the congregation at Willing Workers Missionary Baptist Church in the 90s, you would see me serving in one of these ministries: the mass choir, youth department, drill team, drama team, and more. My life was church, and I enjoyed every bit of it! It was where I felt seen and loved when I felt invisible at home. Many of my gifts and talents were uncovered by others at church, like singing and acting. I spent many days and nights in the choir singing my heart out in all of the beautiful notes of alto. In addition to my ministry at church, I was in a gospel choir called Eternal Life and a group called En Jesus Name. My worship to God was through singing; it was my second language! I stayed busy with ministry and never carved out time for a social life. My church life was my social life. One of my boyfriends and his friends called me "Chapel." They teased me all the time for being "the church girl." I had an extremely close relationship with God, and I leaned on that relationship to help me with my insecurities, lack of self-love, and confidence (another story for another book!). When I went off to college, I stopped going to church, which wasn't an intentional decision; it happened because I didn't drive home every weekend like I thought I would to attend. At first, I would feel bad and guilty about missing church, but the more it happened, the desire to go went away. I was what the old folks would call "a backslider," which means I had gone backward in my spiritual walk with God. I was partying, drinking excessively, and now being "seen" in ways that were not the healthiest for me. I craved love, but I was now looking for it in the wrong places.. I was looking for it in a handsome young man in college. I was lost and seeking validation, so I conformed to what I thought whoever I was entertaining at the time wanted me to be just to feel loved and wanted. That means I was being fake! I dumbed down my truths, morals, standards, and convictions to get those feelings that made my flesh feel good. Sex was one of the biggest convictions that I silenced because I felt like I had to do if I wanted to keep my guy's attention. Heavy feelings of guilt hit me every time I had sex because those teachings from church always resounded in my head. "Your body doesn't belong to you; it belongs to God. No sex before marriage. If he loves you, he will wait." I didn't believe any guy would want me if I shared my standards and convictions. I lacked self-love and self-worth in a major way. It's embarrassing to confess, but it's the truth. My actions were screaming, "I don't love myself! I am not worthy of respect! I don't matter!". I got pregnant, told my family, and then had an abortion (April 1, 1998) during those times. I never thought I would get pregnant at an early age. I knew better from all the talks from church and seeing other young girls go through it. I didn't desire that for myself. I always said if I were to get pregnant, I would NEVER abort the baby. It was against my Christian values, and I didn't think my conscience would allow me to live without the guilt. So how did that happen? I learned at that moment that sometimes circumstances would make you do things you said you would never do. I was head over heels in stupid love. I got comfortable in the relationship, stopped using protection and got pregnant. The guy I was pregnant from threatened to never speak to me again and said I would raise the baby on my own if I chose to have the baby. His exact words were: "I put my life in your hands, and you are f@#&ing it up! Don't call me ever again if you plan to have this baby." I was heartbroken on top of being broken and didn't believe I could parent a child at 19 and alone. To hear the thoughts from my father and my grandmother after I told them I had an abortion was indescribable. I was crushed. I had let down the most important person on earth.. my grandmother. After she expressed her disappointment in me, she expressed major concern about my mental health because she knew having an abortion was something I would not have done. She was right! I was going crazy! How could I abort a baby.. God's creation? So many want this blessing.. On top of that, why did I still love a person who mistreated me? What was wrong with me? Shortly afterward, I flunked out of college. Not because I wasn't brilliant, but because I didn't go to class. I couldn't find the strength and will to do it. I was so depressed. I just wanted to stay in bed and sleep through the nightmare. My world was falling apart, and I had a good idea why. I remember sobbing listening to Boyz II Men's "Doing Just Fine" on repeat while packing up my stuff to leave Sam Houston State. I wanted to be what the words said in the song, but I was far from it. I cried for an entire week because I felt like a disappointment to my family, myself, and God. I couldn't believe this was me.. How could I be so lost and so low in life? I knew better. I was a Christian and knew God.. why didn't that keep me from being in this space? I came back home to Houston and registered for cosmetology school. One year later, I graduated pregnant with Taylor. I was a hot mess, just trying to hold it all together. While at home, I still wasn't going to church like I was before I went off to college. Going to church was so easy years before, but it was now such a challenge. In addition to not going to church, I still did things that I knew wasn't right for me. I was spiraling fast! Two months after having Taylor, I went to a bachelorette party at a male strip club for one of my associates. I ended up frequenting the male strip club every weekend after doing things I had no business doing. Why? I don't know; it was just something fun to do with my friends. The deejay was jamming and I loved to dance freely without men wanting to dance with me every minute like in the "regular" clubs. I liked to drop it like it was hot SOLO! Lol, Even though I felt like nothing was wrong with the environment because I wasn't giving money to the strippers, I felt that tug of conviction from the Holy Spirit in my belly that told me it wasn't what God had for me.

One day, I was in Popeyes Chicken eating with a friend and a lady walked up to us and pointed at me. I slowly looked up at her. She began to speak, "God told me to tell you something. If you don't stop doing whatever it is that you are doing, there will be destruction." Then she walked away. It scared the living hell out of me! I thought to myself, "Was I just prophesied to? Was this accurate? Did God really send her? What was He talking about? Is it the strip club?" To make a long story short, I was disobedient. I made no changes to my lifestyle. A couple of weeks later, a young lady tried to run me over in the parking lot because I talked to "her stripper," who happened to be my friend. A couple of months later, I was at MD Anderson dealing with this "granular cell tumor." I had to give you the back story of my spiritual life to understand how this surgery & recovery challenged me spiritually.

Why Did This Happen?

I felt like this chapter of my life of nearly dying was a punishment from God. I thought He was angry with me because I lived a life that didn't bring Him glory. I was doing whatever made me feel good vs. what He required of me. I wasn't as close to God as before because I felt too ashamed to pray to Him. I mean, I had sinned so much, and I was disobedient. I would pray, but I could feel the distance because I wasn't confessing my sins and receiving God's forgiveness. It's like I was hiding from Him. I just kept the devil's lies circulating in my thoughts and destroying my self-worth and my life literally..

During the recovery phase, I felt like I was faking my praise. As I lifted my hands in gratitude for God healing my body and saving my life, I was frustrated with being in the situation and wanted it to be over. Like, enough is enough, God! Thank you and all, but I need THIS part to be over. It's just too hard! How could I praise God and complain at the same time? I felt guilty, crazy, and ashamed that I thought those thoughts and felt that way. Regardless, I prayed every day, whether it was a good day or a bad day, for God to help me. As I woke up every day, I yearned for God's presence and His power to get through this. I knew first-hand about His power from past experiences in my life. Little by little, I began to confess the heavy baggage of sins that I carried for years in my invisible backpack. The more I confessed, the lighter I felt. The more I confessed, the more I felt the freedom to talk to Him. I questioned him often… "Why did you allow me to go through this?" What will life look like for me after this? Will it always be this exhausting to breathe when I do basic things? How long will it take for me to recover? Why is this so tough?" I told Him my honest thoughts. "You knew it was already challenging for me to love myself; now you have added all of these limitations that make me invaluable. Who is going to love me now? Thank you for loving me. Please help me on this journey." Oh, I had a roller coaster of thoughts that I verbalized to God. I was lying on my back with nothing else to do but talk to God. I was low on faith and hope and didn't know what to do. Then I remembered what the Bible said about faith, that all I needed was a mustard seed to get through this. I planted that mustard seed of faith, and it began to grow! It didn't happen right away, but faith is belief in what I didn't see. Little by little, I began to see the light and gain hope and more faith. I began to believe that I could overcome this hurdle, but only with God. This test would one day be a full testimony if I kept going. It was a grueling journey. However, I leaned on God for everything I needed, whether patience, peace, faith, endurance, determination, or belief in myself... Whatever came up that I was lacking. I had no one to talk to but Him, and we got close again. I stopped feeling guilty about my past mistakes and started receiving God's mercy, love and grace. I truly learned just how much God loved me when I thought I was unlovable. I was fearful, thought I was unattractive, frustrated, wanted to quit, and was discontent about my situation, and God still loved me unconditionally. My perspective of feeling like this was a punishment began to change. This journey was indeed a blessing! In my opinion, Him saving my life was proof that He loved me. Even though I didn't see it right away, God had me in the best position to get things right with Him, get stronger spiritually, and give me a new perspective for my new life.

CHAPTER 9

ONE LUNG TO LIVE

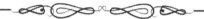

In about five months after I was released from the hospital in Feb. 2001; I was settled and adjusting well to my new body. I was thinner than my average size, but I had a healthier look. I hadn't been out of the house much in five months, but I had set a goal to be up and dancing July 1st for my 23rd b-day party. I did just that! It was time to celebrate in a significant way! Birthdays were always a big deal in my eyes, but now birthdays are EXTRA special! This birthday celebrated many things such as The Blessing of Life, God's Glory, Survival of Life, God's Healing, The Accomplishment of Rehabilitation and what was to come! The party was filled with lots of emotional moments with highlights of fun! I am forever thankful to my family and friends that showed up from all seasons of my life to celebrate.

The next day, I woke up with an immense feeling of accomplishment! I looked around the room like I had never seen it before. This experience altered my lens of life, so everything looked different. The things I took for granted before all of this were now tremendous blessings and reasons to thank God. I thought to myself, "I did it! What I cried, fought and prayed to do, I did with God's help!" I sat and let those thoughts penetrate my spirit. I can walk without a walker or assistance from "nurse" Taylor. Thank You, God! I learned my new moving pace, so it was easier to breathe while walking or doing any movements. Thank You, God! The shower seat was a thing of the past! I was strong enough to bathe myself and get in and out of the tub like a champ! Thank You, God! The 2-pound weights were resting in the closet because my 5-pound weights were my new workout partners. Thank You, God! The biggest smile spread across my face as I now danced around my house without feeling like it was the "last" dance. Thank You, God! If the toilet could talk, it would praise God because I no longer plopped down on it when my knees would get weak in the bend while squatting. Thank You, God! My raspy whisper graduated to a sultry, one-of-a-kind, smooth and raspy tone that I love to hear. Thank You, God! My appetite was back in full effect! I ate full meals and got my normal "hangry" when I didn't get to eat fast enough. Thank You, God! My pillows were NOW only used for my head instead of my butt when I sat down. Thank You, God!!! I still avoided stairs at all costs, but for the most part, I was healed and fully recovered!!

Now it was time to LIVE, even though I didn't quite know how that looked…I needed to figure out what I would do for the rest of my life. By this time, I had been rejected by disability. How was I going to take care of myself and Taylor? Could I even work with such limited physical abilities? My dream had always been to own a hair salon, but was that still my path? What else that I am good at do I like to do? Should I go back to school? I desired to have a family; could I have more babies with one lung? What special man would create a family with me? I had such big dreams for my life; could I still achieve them? What is my reason for existence? So many questions, right? Even though I just about drove myself crazy trying to figure it all out, I knew God had a plan already mapped out for my life that I needed to uncover. It wasn't my place to figure it out; my job was to seek Him daily, trust Him and give Him Glory for it all! Even though there were so many unknowns, what I did know was that He would use my testimony to give Him glory in a major way. I knew there was a profound purpose for my life and this experience! I knew I was the chosen vessel for the ministry of the Holy Spirit to reach someone who needed what I was willing to grow through for a TESTIMONY!

Twenty-One Years Later

Today I sit here still in awe of what God did in Md Anderson and what He has done with my life in the past 21 years. There isn't a word created to describe it, so I will settle with WOOOW!!! I know you wonder what happened, so let me jump right into it!

Health

I am doing exceptionally well! I have not only learned to live with my physical limitations, but I have mastered my new way of life. My lung has expanded to a lung and a half, which means my lung capacity is about 60%. This is a big deal considering that I lost the larger lung. To keep from being winded and out of shape, I do low impact exercises such as walking, dancing, Pilates and light weights to keep my body strong and toned. My diet is plant-based for the most part. I slide some salmon in from time to time (wink). I take a lot of supplements and drink a lot of smoothies!

Yummy! I keep my environment toxin-free to help my respiratory system stay healthy.

I have routine visits to Md Anderson where they do an X-ray and Cat Scan and every four years a bronchoscopy (uugghh I still don't like those.. lol) to make sure the tumor has not returned. Dr. Walsh is still impressive, and every year that I see him, he tells me another story about my stay in Md Anderson that I have never heard before. After 21 years, even he is still stunned by this story. I am eager to see him EVERY year because we share a very particular connection. In March 2020, during our visit, he looked down at his chart and back up at me. He noted that it had been 20 years of seeing him for routine visits without any issues. He then told me the unexpected, "I am discharging you. You don't have to come back again." As exciting as that news was, I was sad. It was a blow that I didn't see coming. I didn't know this would be our last visit, but nothing could have prepared me for it even if I did. I wanted to burst into tears, but I held them back. I wanted to hug him again before I left, which would have been awkward because we typically embraced when he entered the room. It was a bittersweet moment, but it was great news. I just needed time to process it and move forward in another victory. I still deal with the effects of knowing I won't see the Dr. who saved my life again. He will always be God's extraordinary gift to me!

Family

Family is so important to me. I am so glad God had it in His plan to bless me with a family of my own! In 2011, I married my wonderful husband, Christopher Williams. Yes, someone came along and loved and accepted me just as I was with my physical limitations and my uncompromising spiritual walk with God. We have four beautiful children named Tamiah, Taylor, Tre & Cadence. I love them so much! If you are wondering, yes, I gave Dr. Walsh a heart attack by getting pregnant. Lol! I carried each baby to full term and had vaginal deliveries with ONE LUNG without any complications. God is amazing!! Just like Taylor was my "why" back in the day, my whole family is my "why" and motivation today to keep living and fulfilling my purpose! I am so blessed and lucky that He chose these people to be MY family.

Career

It took me some time to work like a "normal" person regarding my energy levels, but when I did, I worked in the banking industry for a couple of years. I love numbers! I did go back to college and after many attempts to get my degree, God revealed that was not His path for me. I struggled with this for a very long time because, in my opinion, a degree was what I needed to be successful, educated and respected by others. There is nothing wrong with getting a degree; however, God planned to allow me to be the example to the world of what a different path of success looks like. I didn't need a degree to complete His assignment for me. I was already equipped with the right tools to impact the world in my unique way. When I let go of society's standards of success and embraced the ultimate success of finding and operating in my purpose, the right doors began to open for me. My passion for hair never went away but grew stronger, so I decided to put my cosmetology license to use and become a full-time hairstylist in 2006. My talents as a hairstylist help women feel and be the very thing I struggled to find..Confidence and Self-worth! It's incredible what a great hairstyle and meaningful conversation can do. On April 1, 2008, I walked into the Harris County Clerk's Office and purchased my DBA for my salon named Euphoric Essence Hair Salon. I took one of the worst days of my life and turned it into one of the best days of my life! Can you believe it? I became an entrepreneur! Euphoric Essence Salon was a dream that came true! In 2013, on a trip for my 35th birthday, I asked God what I needed to do more with my existence. He said, "Tell your story!" On that trip, I told Chris that it would be an excellent idea to walk around with my story on my shirt to be a walking billboard for God's glory. I realized that everyone needed to share their story, so I opened 22 Collectives, an online t-shirt brand that encourages people to tell their stories. I became a Cert. Wellness Coach in 2018 to help myself and others be well in all aspects. After learning about how chemicals in the environment negatively affect health, I decided to create a healthy solution for the haircare industry to keep women beautiful and healthy. In 2020, I launched an online Vegan & Organic Haircare Line named Cadence Taylor Organic Beauty. I have been awarded: 2022 Top 50 Black Professionals & Entrepreneurs of Texas, Best of Sugar Land Awards-Beauty Salon 2019, 2020, 2021 & 2022, Sugar Land Business Hall of Fame 2021 & 2022. As you can see, God had a strategic plan for my life and didn't allow me to use any limitations as an excuse not to get it accomplished. He did it all!

Spiritual Life

I am closer to God now than I have ever been. I feel the closest to Him when I am literally His hands and feet in the form of ministry and service. Ministry used to be something I did at church only. Now I am always doing ministry work at home (my 1st ministry), work, social media, wherever God gives me the nudge to do so. Before the pandemic, I was an active volunteer smiling and giving out listening guides as a greeter at the entrance of New Hope Church, my church home, which is the BEST church ever! I now watch Pastor Tim from my TV online mostly and occasionally go and enjoy church under the pavilion outside. I have grown so much spiritually at New Hope! I am forever thankful to God for leading me to such an awesome place full of genuine, diverse and imperfect people who love God and each other. I miss going to church in person and volunteering so much! I can't wait to go back! I meet on Zoom on Sundays to study the Bible and enjoy my sisters from my Women's Life Group from New Hope Church. I love them! On Facebook, I have another group of sisters in the #Wifelife Ministries. I am the Beauty & Wellness Consultant for that ministry. They are an inspiration to me! I feel like I am right where God wants me to be for Him to continue to use me for His glory.:)

My Purpose

One of the most important blessings from this story is that I found my purpose of living, which is how God uses me to make this world a better place. I inspire and connect with others through my stories. I encourage others to tell their story. I help women obtain beauty and wellness to live a life of self-love, freedom, peace, joy, fulfillment and more! The journey to finding my purpose did not happen overnight and was not easy. I hit plenty of roadblocks, but I kept seeking, and I kept going. I look back at how God connected every piece of the puzzle, which is unimaginable. I can't wait to share that story which might be in the form of another book!

Another critical part of this experience is the lessons learned from this story. I have casually shared the lessons I have learned when prompted in random conversations throughout the years. It's time that I am intentional about my God-given assignment to share the lessons from challenging times of adversity to help others.

CHAPTER 10

LESSONS LEARNED

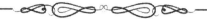

I am glad I went through every part of this journey because it has made me who I am today. All along, I questioned God, asking, "Why am I going through this?" When I should have asked myself, "Why not me?" What made me exempt from being used by God to bring Him glory? I didn't see it at first, but God allowed me to go through that experience to enhance your survival guide of life with the lessons I have learned. It's never been about me; it was about how God used me to help you navigate through life as your best self.

Know God and Make Him Known

The most important thing that I learned from this experience is truly knowing who God is. I knew Him before, but I learned more about His indescribable character. God is genuinely AMAZING in all His ways. Having God in my life as my Lord and Savior has been the best thing I have ever done! Here are some of the ways I got to know God more intimately.

1. God's love is unconditional. I felt God's unconditional love when He healed my body and loved me in the moments that I thought that I was unlovable. As bad as things got for me, I knew they could have been worse if it wasn't for God's unconditional love.

"For I am convinced that neither death nor life, neither angels nor demons, neither the present nor the future, nor any powers, neither height nor depth, nor anything else in all creation, will be able to separate us from the love of God that is in Christ Jesus our Lord."

Romans 8: 38-39

God loves you unconditionally too. No matter what you do or who you are, nothing can separate you from His unconditional love!

2. God performs miracles. It would be an understatement to say that this experience was miraculous. I died two times, lived on a ventilator for over a month, had a lung removed, etc., and

I am sitting here 21 years later, healthy, strong and telling my story. It had to be something greater than mere human strength that performed those miracles that took place.

"You are the God who works wonders; You have made known Your strength among the peoples."

Psalm 77:14

Believe it or not, miracles, like God has performed in my life, are common. He performs miracles every day! It can reveal itself in the form of impossible dreams that come true, unexplained healing, promotions of the "unqualified," or, in its simplest form...being alive. Acknowledge your miracle gifts from God and be thankful!

3. God has healing power. As much as I could give my doctors all the credit for my successful surgery, I know that God worked through them. The transformation of my body while I recovered in ICU, was beyond human comprehension. The only resounding reason for my healing was God! My family and friends prayed for my healing, and God healed me! What an amazing Father I serve!

"This is what the Lord, the God of your father David, says: 'I have heard your prayer and seen your tears; I will heal you."

2 Kings 20:5

I am not the only one that God has healed and will heal. He has healed a multitude of people starting in the Bible. I love to hear stories over and over about God's crazy power of healing! Even though it should be of no surprise, it's always mind-blowing. If you find yourself in a situation where you need His healing, pray and believe God for healing.

4. God forgives. All have sinned and fallen short of the glory of God. Despite my sins, mistakes and failures, God forgave me! I carried things around that caused me stress and worry for too long. I no longer hesitate about going to God to lay everything at His feet and receive His forgiveness.

"If we confess our sins, he is faithful and just to forgive us our sins and to cleanse us from all unrighteousness."

1 John 1:9

Share your honest and transparent thoughts, feelings and actions with God and ask Him to forgive you, and He will. He won't judge you or think any less of you. Stop carrying your invisible baggage of regrets and mistakes; your shoulders and conscience need relief! Stop allowing your past to cripple you from reaching your destiny. Receive God's forgiveness and His peace; He is there for you!

5. God is gracious and merciful. I complained and cried in my moments of frustration because I was borderline angry with God. I was fearful of the result I would get from doing that. I knew it wasn't right to complain or cry out to God in the disappointment of my current circumstance. Instead of giving me what I deserved, He blessed me every day with new mercy just as if it never happened. This characteristic of God made me love Him even more. He gave me the benefit of the doubt by not punishing me but showing me compassion and forgiveness. Thank you, God! In addition to that, I wanted God to bless me with everything I needed, but did I deserve that? What had I done to earn the blessings I asked of Him? Nothing! I learned in that season that I would never "do" enough to deserve or earn anything from God. He is gracious. He gave me blessings on top of blessings that I did not have to work for or earn from Him. He freely gave me love and unmerited favor! Grace! I praise God daily for His grace and mercy! I don't know what I would do without it!

"But in your great mercy, you did not put an end to them or abandon them, for you are a gracious and merciful God."

Nehemiah 9:31

God gives you a new batch of grace and mercy every day, open your heart and soul and receive His gifts. Have you had a hard time giving yourself some compassion for the mistakes you have made in your life? Listen, if God can give you mercy, you can do the same thing for yourself and others. You are not on earth to prove how perfect you can be or to prove to God that you are worthy of the blessings you ask Him for, so release that unrealistic expectation and embrace God's infinite gifts of grace and mercy. Your life will be much more peaceful and joyful. When it comes to others, they will fail you unintentionally because they are human and imperfect. Give them the same mercy you would want to be given to you. Extend grace and kindness to others because life is tough, and everyone needs a break.

6. God is always there. When the phone calls and visits slowed down, I felt like I was all alone, making me very fearful and anxious. I didn't know what to do with myself. After I acknowledged God's presence in everything around me, my anxiety began to go away. I talked to Him in prayer daily, which gave me so much peace and comfort. The reality was, I was never alone. God never left me; He was there to be everything I needed Him to be.

"Have I not commanded you? Be strong and courageous. Do not be afraid; do not be discouraged, for the Lord your God will be with you wherever you go.

Joshua 1:9

This thing called life will take you to some lonely places that make you feel scared, anxious and abandoned. Know that nothing is by chance; it's all part of the plan for you to grow and be a better version of yourself. Know that even in the most challenging times, God is there with you, carrying you the most. He is with you for the long haul. Feel comfort in knowing that you are NEVER alone. Not only are you never alone, but you are accompanied by your Creator, who knows and cares more about you than anyone else. Feel His presence, when the wind blows, when the sun shines, the birds chirp and when it rains.. He is there.

7. God is our strength. It was not in my strength that I made it through everything I went through. I am pretty strong, but not strong enough to do that. It was beyond anything I could ever do. Yes, I now have physical limitations, and I could use them as excuses to not reach the goals and dreams that I have for my life, but I don't because I have God. He has shown me time after time that I do nothing in my own strength. I have tried, but trust me, it doesn't work. I am thankful that I have God to lean on for my strength; it's one of the ways He gets the glory for the things in my life.

"The Lord is my strength and my song; he has given me victory. This is my God, and I will praise him — my father's God, and I will exalt him!" Exodus 15:2

Most things you do and are predestined to do are bigger than what you could ever do in your strength. Stop trying to do it on your own. You need help, and that's ok! Many walk around acting like it is a badge of honor to do things without assistance. Put your pride to the side. It doesn't make you any less of a person because you need help. God created you to need Him. Help from God typically comes in the form of support from others that you may or may not know, so stay open to receiving it. I know people have said they would help you and didn't, or they helped you and threw it back up in your face to put you down for "needing" them. Everyone isn't like that, so let go of those hurtful encounters and move forward in victory. Ask God to be your strength and help, and I guarantee He will be! While you may get weary and weak, God's strength never runs out!

8. God is powerful. God can do ANYTHING! He brought me back from death. I am not just alive, but I am LIVING because of God! There are no limitations on what God has done and continues to do through me because I operate in His power. I am His walking billboard showcasing His limitless and miraculous power.

"But he said to me, 'My grace is sufficient for you, for my power is made perfect in weakness. 'Therefore I will boast all the more gladly of my weakness so that the power of Christ may rest upon me."

2 Corinthians 12:9

There is nothing you can't do with God by your side! Big dreams, visions, crazy goals, etc. should be approached with an enormous sense of Godfidence (confidence in God in you) because you can do it all with God's power! God created you to trust, lean and depend on Him for everything. In your weakness is when God's power shows the most. Allow His power to be made perfect in you!

Be Thankful

"Give thanks in all circumstances; for this is the will of God in Christ Jesus for you."

1 Thessalonians 5:18

Before any of this, I woke up every morning and didn't thank God. I honestly didn't think about doing that. I took that and many other things that "just happen" for granted because God blessed me with it without me asking for it or thinking about it. MY DEFINITION OF BLESSINGS CHANGED when I could not eat, walk, talk, sit on the toilet, and bathe. When I woke up in ICU, I then focused on what a blessing it was to wake up and breathe independently without a ventilator. I no longer took anything for granted. Whether I ask for it or not, everything big and small is considered a BLESSING that I am forever THANKFUL for. Even in the low parts of my journey, being thankful changed my perspective. I began to focus and be grateful for what I had versus what I didn't have. This action helped me to be optimistic.

Reasons to Be Thankful:

1. **Changes your perspective and makes you hopeful.**

2. **Gives you confidence.**

3. **Helps you deal with adversity.**

4. **Promotes positive feelings.**

5. **Builds healthy and strong relationships.**

6. **Opens the door for more blessings.**

It is the will of God for you to be thankful no matter what. Thank God for everything He is and everything He does in your life. When you open your eyes in the morning, move your legs and arms, open your mouth to talk, tell God Thank You, and smile! Do this daily whether you feel like it or not. You will feel great after you fill your heart with gratitude and pour it out to God! If you only woke up with the things you thanked God for, what would you have? Develop your language of gratitude and watch your life change for the better.

Take Care of Your Body

"Or do you not know that your body is a temple of the Holy Spirit within you, whom you have from God? You are not your own, for you were bought with a price. So glorify God in your body."

1 Corinthians 6:19-20

The importance of taking care of my body wasn't something I thought about often because I was reasonably healthy before this experience. I was highly active and LOVED to dance! I realized that the health of my body was vital after having my lung removed. God had given me a second chance in life, and my way of thanking and honoring Him was to take care of my temple. I made adjustments in my lifestyle and learned how to be well in every aspect of my life to preserve my health.

Ways to Stay Healthy

1. **Stay physically well** with a healthy diet, frequent exercise, plenty of rest, deep breathing exercises and consistent visits to the doctor.

2. **Stay mentally and emotionally well** with positive thoughts, affirmations, journaling and more.

3. **Stay spiritually well** with prayer, mediation, devotions and reading the Bible.

4. **Stay environmentally well** by removing all harmful toxins from what you inhale and put on your skin.

5. **Stay social well** by spending time around those who love and value you. Have some fun!

6. **Stay intellectually well** by reading often or learning something new.

God has blessed you with a vehicle to move around on earth, also known as your healthy body. Your body is like your car. Cars last longer and run well when you keep up with their maintenance. When you see old cars that are still in good shape, you typically say, "Oh, they took care of that car." When you borrow a car, you take care of it because it doesn't belong to you and you want to return it in excellent condition. As you see in the scripture above, you don't own your body; God does. Glorify and thank God for every part of it by taking care of it. These things are essential because you have to be in good health to fulfill your reason for existence on earth. Your health is truly your wealth!

Tell Your Story

"I will speak of Your testimonies also before kings, And will not be ashamed."

Psalm 119:46

I used to be ashamed to share anything about myself that didn't show me in a positive light. I feared being talked about negatively and being judged. After this story took place, I started to share it unintentionally when people would notice how slow I walked or why I needed to catch my breath after minimal physical exertion. The response I got was shocking and overwhelming. Some people couldn't hold back their river of tears, others let their mouths hang open in disbelief, and some told me that my story was a blessing to them. I realized that I was supposed to be intentional about sharing my testimony; it's one of the main reasons for my existence.

Soon after, I learned that I was supposed to share that testimony and other stories in my life to give God glory. The story that I shared about having an abortion wasn't something I was willing to share for a long time because I felt judged and condemned. I had my judgmental thoughts of someone that had an abortion before I had one. My perspective changed when I found myself in those same shoes. After I completely healed from it mentally and spiritually, I began to open up about it to other young women who I would witness in a sad and embarrassing state from going through the same thing. As I slowly opened up to others, the space that I thought would hold judgment and unfair assumptions had compassion, healing and understanding. It wasn't easy at first to share the stories that I once feared being judged for, but the result of impacted lives was pleasing to God. It turns out others shared the same experiences as I did. I no longer had to seem like I had it all together. The more I shared my stories; I began to experience true genuine connection. I slowly took my "perfect patty" cape off because the more imperfections I exposed, the more I felt inclusive, seen and relatable. As I shared my stories, people felt safe enough to share their stories with me. Most people look nothing like what they have been through, so the more stories I heard, the more I was intrigued by God's unique creations (people). There is always a reason why people behave the way they do and have a certain perspective of life. That reason is always found smack dab in the middle of their story. Sharing my story and listening to others' stories has enriched many lives through connection, inspiration and empowerment. When I encounter a challenging moment, a story of inspiration either from my own story, the Bible, or someone else's story reminds me of God's power that is accessible to me to be victorious. God gets the glory for my testimonies!

Reasons to Tell Your Story:

1. It gives God glory.

2. It inspires others along their journey.

3. It promotes genuine connection and healing.

4. It shares lessons that will help others.

5. It increases compassion and lessens judgment and assumptions.

News flash, your story is meant to change lives! Yes, even the most embarrassing parts are supposed to be shared in the right audience and at the right time. Do you feel uneasy about sharing it? If so, I truly understand your stance. However, I encourage you to get comfortable with sharing. Your story is what makes you unique and set apart from anyone else on earth! Tell your story; it's an invaluable part of you that is meant to change your life and the lives of others! Remember, don't judge someone else by their cover or assumptions you have of them. Take the time to read their pages; most of the time, your beliefs are far from the truth.

Embrace Adversity, It's a Part of the Plan

"And we know that all things work together for good to them that love God, to them who are the called according to his purpose."

Romans 8:28

Before this story, I struggled to deal with adversity in the form of regret for past mistakes and decisions. I wanted to omit parts of my story because I was ashamed of them. I love Taylor with all of my heart. However, one chapter of adversity that I regretted was becoming a mother at such a young age without being married. My family was so disappointed in me when I got pregnant with Taylor. Most importantly, I was disappointed in myself because I had a plan for my life, and it didn't include getting pregnant again at the age of 20. It was challenging to accept such a huge responsibility that I knew I wasn't ready for. That adversity, or what I considered a "mistake," ended up being very significant in this story in more ways than one. Taylor ended up being my biggest blessing in many ways. She made me a better person. She taught me how to love and be unselfish. Her existence saved my life! She was my "why" and the reason that made me fight so hard to live. I love her so much! I honestly don't know if I would be here today if I didn't have that solid motherly instinct to survive to take care of her. Taylor's existence also gave me an unexpected financial blessing! While in the hospital, I was covered by my dad's insurance because I was a full-time college student. When January came, I was still in the hospital, so I obviously couldn't be in school as a full-time student. The insurance company dropped their coverage, so I was no longer insured. Here I was with over a million dollars of hospital bills that needed to be paid, and I was on my death bed with no way to pay them. My mother was able to get me approved for Medicaid, and praise God they took care of my medical expenses! What does Taylor have to do with this? To get approved by Medicaid, I had to be a mother! Taylor's existence was all a part of God's perfect plan for my life. God is so good to me! I no longer question the bad things that happen in my life. Whether it comes out immediately or years later, there is a good reason that God allowed it to happen.

Reasons to Embrace Adversity:

1. **Adversity brings you closer to God.**

2. **Adversity makes you stronger.**

3. **Adversity reveals your purpose.**

4. **Adversity makes you grow.**

5. **Adversity builds character.**

6. **Adversity changes your mindset.**

7. **Adversity gives God glory.**

8. **Adversity is a blessing.**

9. **Something good always comes from adversity.**

God's perfect plan for your life is sprinkled with heartbreaks, setbacks, tragedies, family issues and more. Right now, you may be dealing with emotional, financial and health challenges from the pandemic, divorce, the death of a loved one, or a relationship crisis. These complex parts of life may take you to a low place or maybe even depression, and that's ok. It's ok not to always be ok, so cancel the act of perfection. We all go through these things. The danger comes when you stay in that place for far too long. When things happen in life, know it's for reasons that God intends to use for good at some point in your journey. Nothing happens by chance; it's all a part of the plan and the process to prepare you for the blessings that God has in store for you. Pray and ask God, "What am I supposed to learn from this? How do you intend for me to grow through this?" Sometimes the things you go through produce lessons that add to your survival guide that you are meant to share with others. It's not always just about you; it's about how God can use you as a vessel to help someone else; that's why you exist. I know it's hard, but don't park yourself at the place of pain and hard times because it's all for a good reason. Remember who you are! You are a child of God! You are amazing! You are a survivor! You are an overcomer! You are resilient! You are strong! You are blessed! You are built for this! It's time for you to get up and keep going because your "Good" is on the other side of your adversity. God is there to help you every step of the way. Lean on Him for everything you need! Life is so much sweeter just knowing that God's plan for your life is for GOOD!

Ways to Overcome Adversity:

1. **Understand that everything happens for a reason; find the lesson and the blessing.**

2. **Pray (talk to God) daily.**

3. Ask God for what you need. He promised to supply all of your needs, and He does.

4. Read the Bible or devotional daily.

5. Meditate (listen to God) in silence daily.

6. Believe that things will get better no matter what they look like.

7. Don't isolate yourself from the world. Be transparent with someone you trust so they can encourage you and pray for you.

8. Take each day as it comes to avoid being overwhelmed.

9. Be patient with yourself.

10. Practice gratitude daily.

11. Don't give up no matter how you feel.

12. Remember, something good will come from it.

13. Keep your thoughts positive.

14. Create a plan of action and execute it with consistency.

15. Remember your "why"; it motivates you to keep going.

"For I know the plans I have for you," declares the Lord, "plans to prosper you and not to harm you, plans to give you hope and a future."

Jeremiah 29:11

Stop Comparing Yourself to Others

"For am I now seeking the approval of man, or of God? Or am I trying to please man? If I were still trying to please man, I would not be a servant of Christ."

Galatians 1:10

When I was recovering, I put lots of unnecessary pressure on myself to do it quickly to catch up to the people who were my age. I didn't feel like it was ok to be in that state for too long, so I tried to rush through my recovery. My friends were out there living their best lives, and I was lying in a bed, unable to take care of myself. I also didn't like my new body, scars and life adjustments because they made me stand out in a wrong way, so I thought. I didn't want to seem flawed in any way. In my eyes, this experience was a setback that took me away from fitting in and being accepted by society. I was sad about what I couldn't do vs. what everyone else could do. My self-esteem was low because I didn't look like such and such or do what they were doing. That comparison stole my joy every day until I started seeing the improvements in myself and being thankful for what I could do and how it made me different. I began to compare myself to myself in my day-to-day progress, which showed me I was getting better each day. I began to see and cherish the beauty in my scars. It brought me joy that God would think that much of me to leave evidence of His healing on my body that marked me as a survivor. I started to believe in myself and appreciate my journey. I began to embrace being different. I no longer wanted to fit in and be like everyone else. The imperfections that made me stand out turned into my superpower; it's what made me uncommon and set me apart. Why did I feel the need to compare myself to others? I have no idea. God's path for me doesn't look identical to anyone else's journey because it is specifically made just for me.

Reasons to Stop Comparing Yourself to Others:

1. **It's an insult to God's most precious creation.. YOU.**

2. **You are not made to fit in or be like anyone else.**

3. **Comparison steals your joy.**

Do you compare yourself to others? You can be scrolling on social media and see all the highlight reels of someone else's marriage, friend groups, lifestyle, etc. You feel the need to compare yourself to what you see. Don't let it happen! Comparing yourself to someone else never ends well. There is one original copy of you, and that is YOU. If you didn't know, you are the best thing since sliced bread (as the old folks say)! You are an incredible human being! You bring out the best in other people! You are brave! You are enough! You are perfect just the way you are! You make a difference in this world! You are a gift to those around you! No one can do anything like YOU do it! You are special! What you don't like about yourself is what makes you intriguing. Don't let the "world's" standards make you feel like you are not worthy or valuable because you don't look a certain way, have certain things, or are not doing things in the "right" timing. These things above pertain to losing weight, gaining weight, having children, getting married, buying a house, getting a degree, business success, etc. God created a custom timeline for your life that is perfect. In God's time, things will happen and trust me, it will be well worth the wait. Your job is to be patient, get prepared, remember who YOU are, and run your race with your blinders on in your lane.

Live Intentionally

The average person hasn't faced a tragic experience, let alone at a young age. I hear the phrase "life is short" all the time. After this encounter, it took on real meaning for me. Life was no longer the same. I was not comfortable with just letting life happen to me, I had a second chance at it, and I was going to be intentional about my gift. All this time, I had focused on what I didn't want my life to be like that I didn't know what I wanted. It was time to make a change. I began to pray and seek God about His plan for my life and how to obtain it. I desired a quality life full of my passions, purpose, happiness, holiness, peace, and more, so I intentionally put a plan together to reach my goals. Here are some ways to live intentionally.

Ways to Live Intentionally:

1. Accept Jesus Christ as your personal Savior.

2. Allow God to lead and guide your life.

3. Find your purpose; it brings true joy and fulfillment.

4. Get to know yourself and fall in love with who you are.

5. Do things that bring you joy.

6. Affirm yourself daily.

7. Know when to let go of things that no longer serve you. People, places and things are there for a season, reason, or a lifetime.

8. Surround yourself with people that love, support and help you be the best version of yourself.

9. Self-reflect often; it shows you what areas need growth and what growth to celebrate.

10. Practice Self Care.

11. Celebrate small and big wins! (Yours & Others)

12. Take care of your overall wellness.

13. Find ways to be of service to God and others.

14. Give to others without expectation.

15. Practice gratitude.

16. Forgive yourself and others quickly.

17. Be present in the moment. Put your phone down.

18. Become one with nature.

19. Choose happiness every day.

20. Be consistent in the small things; they reap big rewards.

21. Be kind; you never know what others are going through.

22. Learn how to communicate through and resolve conflict; it's inevitable.

23. Write your vision, make a plan and take action; it's how you reach your goals.

24. Create healthy boundaries for yourself to avoid burnout.

25. Create a daily routine that helps you show up as your best self.

Do you wake up every day and let life just happen to you? Do you have a vision of your desired life? Do you know how you want to show up daily? Have you written it down? A life without being intentional about what you do with it is just life. Life lived with intention is LIVING, and that's what you deserve. Pray and ask God to align your desires with His will for your life. Get clear about what you want in your life. How do you want to feel, what do you want to accomplish, and what kind of person do you want to be? Consistently do the things that energize and awaken your self-love and positive mindset. Small intentional things add up to a life of fulfillment where you wake up every day with a feeling of joy. Start your journey of living intentionally right now! You deserve all of the goodness coming your way!!

Conclusion

God's healing power is the only reason I am here today to share my story, and I hope you were inspired by it. I shared my story with you to change your life with a clear image of God's character, a positive shift in perspective, comfort in knowing you can do anything in God's strength and power, life lessons, and a brighter outlook on adversity.

You will go through adversity and challenging times, not always because you are being punished for something you did wrong, or you are a terrible person. You will go through troubling times because God is trying to get closer to you, reveal your purpose, change you for the better and use you to help others for His glory. During hard times get thankful, pray and seek God, believe you can get through it, find the lesson and give God credit. Remember, it's temporary, and you will be better on the other side of it; just don't quit! You have to reach the mind-blowing destiny that God has for you; this is preparation for you to receive it! After overcoming adversity, it becomes a blessing (story) that you can share with others to help them along their journey. They will feel better knowing that they are not the only person who has gone through what they are experiencing, giving them a sense of hope. A couple of other ways you help others and yourself when you share your story is through connection and inspiration that most people crave to feel seen, valued and loved. Everyone wants this! During adversity, you will learn many lessons that become the keys that unlock someone else's next level of God's plan for their lives. So be intentional, not just with sharing your story but also with your life.

Each breath you take is a miracle, and each day you wake up is a blessing, don't take it for granted. You have a day you were born and a day that you leave this earth. What are you doing in the dash? Fill your life daily with purpose, passions, healthy habits and routines that help you achieve consistent growth and an overall balance of wellness (spiritual, physical, mental, environmental, financial, social, emotional) and happiness.

Be thankful for everything in your life because God has blessed you with it, and it doesn't belong to you (even your body).

You are never alone through the ups and downs that you will encounter. God is always there to be everything you need to overcome every time. Trust

God, pray to Him, believe in Him and enjoy your unpredictable path to greatness!

Lastly, but not least, remember that you are here for a reason! You are loved, valued, worthy, strong and powerful! Your existence makes this world a better place!

I love you!

"Tell Your Story; It Changes Lives!"

Tashell

P.S. If you enjoyed this book, please tell your family and friends about it and leave me a review on Amazon.com. It will help new readers discover my book!

Thank you in advance!

Congratulations!

You have finished my book!!! I am a big giver so I have a Gift to help you start Living Intentionally!

After experiencing many times of depression and being in the dumps from life's circumstances, I have figured out a solid solution that helps me spend less time in those low places and more time enjoying life!

Scan this QR Code and Download My Free Guide:

Ditch the Dumps: A Step-by-Step Daily Routine to Promote a Good Mood and Productive Day

Acknowledgments

To My Lord and Savior Jesus Christ,

We did it! I can't believe you had this planned all along. As you reveal my life to me little by little, I am still mind-blown after all of these years. I hope I make you proud with this book, and I incorporated everything you led me to say. Thank you for being my EVERYTHING! Thank you for healing my body 21 years ago so that I could still be here, giving you glory and changing lives with this miraculous story. Thank you for helping me grow into the Tashell that I am today that's flawed and imperfect, but in love with who you made me to be. Thank you for being there to remind me that I operated through your strength and boldness when I had Imposter's Syndrome while writing this book. You are always there to encourage me in times of doubt. I could go on and on.. You know what it is God.. You know your daughter. I love you more than anything in this world! Thank you for choosing me to be a vessel to help more people know who you are.

To My Loving Husband Christopher,

Thank you for loving me and accepting me just as I am. Thank you for giving me the freedom to grow and evolve into who I am today. You have a gentle way of sharpening me that lets me always know how much you care about me and my assignment on this earth. Thank you for challenging me to do better and dig deeper, especially while writing this book! I love you!

To My Heartbeats,

Tamiah, you have grown so much, and I have enjoyed watching you spread your pretty wings! Your willingness to try new things reminds me to do something even when I am afraid! Keep LIVING courageously! You inspire me to keep trying to be a plant momma... lol (inside joke) #wellnessbeauty

Taylor, you are so creative and hardworking! Your free spirit and beautiful smile remind me to LIVE and not take life so seriously. I need that.. You are beautiful inside and out! Keep shining and shifting the room with your presence! #beauty&brains

Tre, you are so dependable and responsible! You have a way of showing your loving heart without saying much. Thank you for being the first person to sit and listen to me read each chapter I completed when I knew you wanted to be playing your games. Lol, Keep being amazing, son. #reallifeteddybear #myprotector

Cadence, you are sweet, kind and silly! No one makes me laugh as much as you do! The permanent smile that you wear when you dance around all day reminds me to find joy in everything. Keep pushing limits and breaking barriers! #dancingdoll

To My Momma & Daddy (Hermann & Raynola Miles),

Momma, (deep breath) I look back and wonder how you did it, how you went through such a scary and uncertain time with me. I know God was your strength; however, I know it was still challenging. I could not imagine what was going through your mind or the amount of stress you carried at that time. Thank you for your sacrifice! I know I only know half of what you sacrificed during that time to help me fight for my life and recover. I know you quit your job to be at the hospital around the clock with me. I know you spent many nights sleeping in the waiting room and being awakened to doctors in white coats walking around delivering bad news, hoping they didn't come your way. I know you and daddy tag-teamed with the car in valet, so you could go home, take a bath and come right back to the hospital. You sacrificed being a present mother to my other three siblings and a wife to daddy. Thank you for your protection! I know you were the gatekeeper of my room, guarding the sacred space in which you knew I would be healed. You were persistent with the staff to ensure I had the best care during my stay at MD Anderson. You made sure I had my music playing on my ears for inspiration and hope. Thank you for your faith and prayers! You prayed and believed that God would heal me. He heard your prayers, and thank God it was in His will to do just that! Thank you for never leaving my side! You being in the room with me every day made me feel like I could make it because I had you to love me to LIFE! I am thankful for the fight in you! You don't back down easily, so when I was in the battle of my life, you and God were the perfect partners to have in my corner. Momma, I can never thank you enough for what you did for me. I will spend the rest of my life trying to. I love you!

Daddy, thank you for your love and sacrifices! Momma told me the other day about you getting off work and coming straight to the hospital to sit with me so that she could go home. She told me that there was never a time that I was at the hospital alone. If she wasn't there, you were there. Thank you for always being there for me! I had no clue that you were so present at the hospital because I can't remember a lot, and I saw momma's face primarily when I came out of the coma. As I have gotten older and have a family of my own, I can imagine my sickness's effects on the entire household. Thank you for EVERYTHING! I don't take any of it for granted! I love you!

To My Dad & Step-Mom (Jerome & Rhoda Harris),

Thank you both for your love, prayers of healing and support of me! You both have made me a stronger person, and for that, I am grateful! I love you both!

To My Grandmother,

Thank you for your love and your prayers. Thank you for taking such good care of Taylor while I was in the hospital.:) Thank you for being patient with me and giving me the tough love and sternness I needed to recover. Thank you for EVERYTHING! I love you!

To My Aunts,

Aunt Vee, thank you for coming to visit me every day. As scary as that was for you, your love for me outweighed that, so you did it anyway. Thank you for your prayers! Thank you for your sacrifice!

Aunt Kim, thank you for checking on me all the time. Thank you for your good food that helped me get stronger every day. Thank you for taking down my braids after I got home.:) I know I looked a mess! Lol

Thank you both for filling in the gap for whatever was needed for my parents and me. I love you both!

To My Siblings,

I know you all were young children at the time, but thank you all for understanding during my sickness, which altered your everyday life. Thank you all for your love and support! I love you all!

To My Closest Friends,

Lyn, Ericka, Gabby, Vonda, Ashley, Kimbrough, Heather, Aisha, Tunisha, LaQuette, Misty, Alana, Candy, Michael, Jerome and Warren.. We may not talk often, but you all hold a special place in my heart.

Lyn, Gabby, Aisha, Candy, Michael, and Warren, I give an extra special thanks to you all for being there 21 years ago, praying for me to pull through! I know it was frightening for you all to experience, but GOD had a perfect plan that included my healing! Thank God!

Thank you all for your love and support of me! Thank you all for matching my efforts in maintaining a nurturing relationship with you. Thank you all for truly knowing me and handling me accordingly. Thank you all for NOT being a "yes" friend, but telling me the truth at all times, which has driven me to grow in ways I couldn't imagine. Thank you all for being there through the hard times and the good times. Thank you all for the laughs, tears and prayers. You all make me feel safe, which has been challenging to find in friendships. Thank each one of you for being you! You all enrich my life in many ways! I am so ready to celebrate with you all in true Tashell fashion… Music and dancing!

To Dr. Walsh,

…..I am trying to put this into words.. Thank you for being the vessel God used to extend my time on this earth! Thank you for providing the BEST care to me for the past 21 years! You set the standard of how all doctors should be. I get excited thinking about all the lives you enhance or/and save at Md Anderson. God has given you a gift, and you use it to the best of your ability! I know He is proud!

To The Staff at MD Anderson,

Dr. Walsh is excellent. However, I know it takes a team to save lives! God couldn't have picked a better place or a more perfect team to nurture me back to good health. Thank you to the doctors, nurses, assistants, nurse practitioners, respiratory therapists, aids... EVERYONE for working together and giving me the care that goes beyond a paycheck. I was privileged to experience true and genuine love and prayers from my medical providers. Md Anderson's reputation speaks for itself. Everyone there cares about their patients like they are their family. I can't thank you enough for what you all did for me! I love you all!

To Pastor James C. Carrington Jr. & The Willing Workers Baptist Church Family,

Thank you, Pastor Carrington, for coming to visit me in the hospital, giving prayers, love and support to my family and me! Thank you for your teachings. They are the foundation of who I am today.

Thank you all for your continuous prayers of healing during that time. I love you all!

To my Family, Friends and Neighbors,

Thank you all for your prayers, love and support! I couldn't have made it through this without you! I am forever grateful for every one of you!

Made in the USA
Columbia, SC
05 March 2025

54690017R00067